From Prison To Power To Peace

Turning My Setbacks into Comebacks

Felicia L. Pollard

This book is dedicated to my loving husband, my king and my best friend. I honor you today. I know today is a reflection day and I continue to thank God for you being in my life. Thank you for all you do to care for me and the family. Thanks for allowing me to be me and always giving me your unwavering support. Most of all thanks for loving me no matter what! I love you forever.

Table of Contents

Introduction	i
Growing Up	1
They called it SLRD	13
Moving Into Life	18
On the Road to Prison	39
Go Walk in Your Purpose	51
Free Yourself from Confinement	56
Conclusion	59

Acknowledgements

GOD

Today, I want to honor and thank everyone who has loved, supported and been there for me unconditionally. I would like to thank my family, beginning with my parents Emory and Charlie Lewis for your unwavering love and support, my siblings, Charles Rayfield (Kim) Lewis and Valencia Lewis (Myron) Mills and all of my nieces, nephews and cousins. To My extended families, the Irving, thank you for giving me my foundation of God and love of family. Thank you to the Lewis and Pollard families for teaching me how to laugh and enjoy life by coming together. Thank you to John and Rosie Smith, and the entire Dudley family for allowing me to use my gift in cosmetology. Terrie Clawson I appreciate the guidance and contributions in my life and Apostle Terrell Murphy for their spiritual leadership as a spiritual father I honor you and the entire Life Center International family. Margo Wade and Maria Bristol -Reed thanks for keeping me spiritually covered through prayers and words of encouragement this process. To the entire InnerVision Inc. NC family, you have allowed me to learn more about my life and my mental health, for that I thank you. I want to send a special thank you to Tacquise Davis and the Western Carolina University family for believing in me, encouraging me and giving me an opportunity that has changed my life. To Mrs. Vanessa

Gilcreast, I appreciate all you have been in my life and contributions. Patricia and Charles McDaniel for keeping me together, Anja Sutton, and Denise Wiggins thank you for being true friends since elementary. A special thanks to Sha'Toya Johnson for edits and contributions. Thanks also to, Will Hall and Minnie Daniels that always nuggets of wisdom and love. To all of my God parents and God Children with me, I appreciate all the wisdom and guidance you share. To my Special Sisters, Natoya Lewis Brown (RIP) and Malane Angosisye, LaJuan Stevens and Pam Q. Reynolds. I want to thank my wardrobe coordinator, Tammy Terrell, my cover photo and graphic designer Andre Michael. I thank God for all my childhood friends that are still in my life whether it is thru social media or just a simple phone call. I also want to thank all the people that have been there and I did not mention I want to include you too. I send love to all the people that have been angels in my life where they were there for me on certain parts of my journey. I also ask for forgiveness for any that I have wronged because of a sickness and addiction in my journey, from my heart I apologize. I understand that I would not be here without you.

Foreword

More than once, I've heard people say, you can't judge a book by its cover. There's much truth in this expression because you never know the true contents of a book until you open and read it. Likewise, we don't really know the real character of a person until we've gotten acquainted with them because you can only see, in another person, what's already in you.

Thus, all too often, we misjudge and categorize people based solely on appearance, an indication of shallow and limited thinking. It's best to follow the biblical expression that says, "A tree is known by the fruit that it bears." When I met Felicia in the early 1990s, she already had plenty of fruit on her tree. She was a successful, board certified cosmetologist with a beautiful clientele, and gave off not the slightest indication, that she would ever become a convicted felon who would eventually do hard time for crimes, most often associated with young black males.

She was talented, gifted, knowledgeable, successful, holder of a state-issued cosmetology license and blessed with a pleasing personality that was as real on the outside as it was on the inside. So it really didn't bother me when I learned about her time behind bars. For me, coming from a bad situation to a good situation is a good thing and always cause for celebration because many people, especially prison bound, are never able to turn a setback into a comeback.

Felicia rode a hell- bound train, straight down to the deepest parts of hell, and decided, once there, that it was not where she belonged. Invoking the spirit of the celebrated human rights activists, Fannie Lou Hamer, she declared, "I am sick and tired of being sick and tired", and then made an irrevocable decision that she and hell simply were not meant for each other.

So she did what all champions do when they get knocked down: she got back up, got back on that train and role it straight outta hell! Prison does strange things to people, some good--- some bad, the same with drugs. In this startling narrative from, *Prison to Power to Peace*, Felicia's nightmarish journey and decent into near madness is an electrifying portrait of love, faith, hope, redemption, self-discovery, self-renewal and atonement.

Indeed, in reading Prison *to Power to Peace*, you will surely feel her pain, but it's hardly a downer because she shines a light that glows brighter with every passing page. Let this book and her story be a blessing to someone you love, someone you admire… someone in need of a mega dose of inspiration, restoration, and perpetual joy. In the end, she's telling us that true love, agape love, is the real answer for all the challenges we face, and that love of self, is the greatest love of all. Let Felicia show you some love, then be a lighting bug and go light up somebody's life.

----John Raye,
Kernersville, NC, May 2016

Our Deepest Fears

"Our deepest fear is not that
we are inadequate.
Our deepest fear in that we are
powerful beyond measure.
It is our Light, not our
Darkness, that most frightens
us.
We ask ourselves, who am I to
be brilliant, gorgeous, talented,
and fabulous?
Actually, who are you not to
be?
You are a child of God. Your
playing small does not serve
the World.
There is nothing enlightening
about shrinking
so that other people won't feel
insecure around you.

We were born to make manifest the glory of God that is within us.
It is not just in some of us; it is in everyone.
As we let our own Light shine, we consciously give other people permission to do the same.
As we are liberated from our own fear,
our presence automatically liberates others."

Marianne Williamson
Return to Love

Introduction

Today, I am grateful for all of the experiences, circumstances, and issues of my past. I give God all the honor and praise for my journey and opening my eyes to the possibilities. I live free and with the power of God. I live in peace, purpose, and with an abundance of prosperity.

As I ponder about what I desire for one who reads this book, I think about my beginning. The labels we sometimes allow others to place on us and how those labels direct our lives. I look at the choices we make to please others, to avoid the pain and judgement by people we thought were part of our circle and our safe haven. The first gem I will give you is when people show you themselves, believe them and then govern yourself accordingly. Even in that pain, one learns to endure it and allow it to lead them to God, thus being empowered to continue to change the negatives into positives.

In the end, the answers that you need are hidden deep in your consciousness and you do not need to look for answers about yourself anywhere else. You will learn to control your heart and consciousness then break free from the imprisonment of your mind.

My hope is that in the context of this book you can find answers to some of the least common yet most important questions to living with purpose. I pray that you find answers to some of the queries that you have and you find some of the answers that you need in order to discover your peace and your power. I also hope that you recognize who you are and what your possibilities are in this world.

This book is the beginning of a series that will help to reveal how you can find the secrets that are within you, reveal the doubts that you have about your purpose, and to share my journey and wisdom with you. Through uncovering secrets, finding my purpose and experiencing life, I've taken negative situations, negative environments and turned them into a positive and productive life.

People may say that it is easy to break free from an imprisoned mind. It is not that easy to control your mind or your heart. It is challenging but the one thing that you should not do is to doubt that there is a treasure of knowledge and great wisdom that exists within your heart. You have the power to break free. You have the courage to look inside and discover the person you are meant to be.

We change with course of time. It's the experiences that you use to access your wisdom that catapults you in the direction of your destination and sets you free. You are already the person you want to be, the only thing you need to do is to see it for yourself. You need to prepare yourself and make yourself strong enough to believe that you have the ability to bend the bar and remove all of the obstacles in your way then you can access the treasure of wisdom that you hold.

I thank God for both the positive and negative experiences. Each experience has provided lessons from which I now govern my life. I aspire to continue to grow through my relationship with God. May you dig deep and discover the highest power that guides you through any situation.

Throughout this book there are opportunities to journal and record your thoughts. Please use this book to find your truth, grow through your journey and watch your growth over the years. It is my wish that this book becomes a reference for your life.

-May His grace guide you-

My abilities are:

_____
_____
_____
_____

I think my obstacles are:

_____
_____
_____
_____

(How many are self-inflicted?)

I believe my destiny is:
_____
_____
_____
_____
_____

Chapter 1:

Finding an Outlet

Growing Up

> Train up a child in the way he should go; even when he is old he will not depart from it.
> Proverbs 22:6

Usually when people hear the name Cook County Hospital they think of the television show ER. The show was based on this hospital. Cook County is my beginning. Midnight had fallen on the Westside of Chicago and it was time for my debut. I came into the world as a fighter. It was in October, 90 days before my supposed due date and I weighed just over three pounds. The doctor sat down with my parents to inform them that my chances of survival were slim. Laying in an incubator, I was the size of an Idaho potato and as fragile as a butterfly fresh from the cocoon but God had great plans for my life.

Cook County became my home away from home for the next three months. The doctors watched me carefully making sure that my lungs completely developed. My mother spent every day at the hospital creating a bond that has never been broken.

Despite a challenging beginning my mother said I was a strong, talented and healthy child. She did not treat me any different than my older brother. I believe my mother recognized my gifts as I grew older. At around the age of 3 my mother signed me up for dance and other activities that kept my brain busy which was turned on 24/7. Mother noticed that when I danced that all was well.

All frustrations, pain, sadness, loneliness and anxiety melted away when I would dance. My mother saw the joy when others could only see a troubled and challenged child. She allowed me to be fully expressive through my dance. One of my favorite things to say to my mother was "I'm bored".

I learned as an adult that boredom was my desire to have an outlet to express my creativity. Mother understood. She knew that I needed to stay busy. She chose to enroll me in girl scouts, dancing, afterschool programs, and summer youth programs. This was the ticket, the answer. Dancing gave me the opportunity to participate, to perform and provided me a sense of peace within. It was one of my creative outlets.

At about three years of age we moved to Maryland this is where my love for dance developed, leading to me a group of girls who like me loved to dance. That's when we came together and formed a group called "Tiny Bubbles". We danced for a band called "Hot Property." We started off as four young ladies, around 12 years of age and were extremely popular traveling around the DMV area but somewhere down the line a decision was made to make additions to the group. After about four or five years the decision was made to make additions to the group. This was a trigger of rejection that led me to question my own abilities and affected my direction and my path. This was the first time I questioned if I was good enough.

Being part of the Tiny Bubbles was a great experience. Not only was dancing an outlet for my energy but I also realized at that point, dancing was a place of peace for me. It gave me the opportunity to perform as I battled low self-esteem, a lack of self-awareness and thoughts that I was not or could not be good enough. In dancing, I found joy that remains part of my life today. When hurt, pain, or stress comes in to my life dance is where I go to escape. The Tiny Bubbles allowed me to do one thing that brings me joy and a sense of peace. I also gained lasting friendships and that was important to me, the girls became like an extension of family, we spent a lot of time together.

Because of what I learned when reading Lisa Nichols book "Abundance Now" there are different types of friendship encountered during our lives. For that reason I look forward to the next Tiny Bubbles reunion.

My true friends are:

_____
_____
_____
_____

One of our chaperons that traveled with the group became my traveling mom. Whatever she and her daughter did, I did. Where they went, I went. They embraced me as one of their own. They took me to special events, allowing me to engage in so many different experiences that were a very positive influence in my life. It was an amazing experience as a child to have your growth stimulated through another person's experiences. As a child I lacked the understanding to properly appreciate those experiences, but I look back now and I clearly see the changes, the goals and the influence of the Tiny Bubbles and experiences it allowed me. In high school, a young man pointed out that we were no longer the "Tiny Bubbles" but the "Big Bubbles".

He was right. As we grow things change and change is not always a smooth or easy transition. This was true even with the Tiny Bubbles. In the group, there were moments where peace seems to have left us and the bubbles were about to burst; nevertheless, though friendships were bruised they were intact. The changes in the dynamics of our group had a very negative effect on my future relationships with women. I believe it became the moment that ended my relationships with groups of women. I am still cautious when I am part of a group that is mostly women. That experience taught me to be aware and watch my circle and if necessary plan my exit strategy. The fears that developed within me and caused the hurt of feeling pushed away is very much alive in me. It was then that I lost my innocence and became bound.

An ancient belief states that a new born child is perfect in every manner of life and we spend our entire lives trying to return to that level of perfection and innocence. At the time of birth, a child is pure, a baby does not know fear, and they are innocent, having limitless abilities for anything, they are only bound to the creator of the world. A young child loves the wonders of life and lives life to its fullest. At that age you were truly a light, you were bound to nothing and had unlimited potential to reach anything.

Most of us lose this natural ability with increasing age and we lose the greatest gift that we were born with, which is the gift to love and to be loved. Somewhere along the way we lose our natural innocence and become someone conditioned by circumstances we have encountered through our environment.

This behavior does not represent the natural human characteristics. It is a result of what we become after we leave the natural innocence behind us. We begin to spend our days in the world carelessly because of our wounds that we have received through the experiences in our lives. We question our circumstances and how we find ourselves in our current lives. The first place to seek understanding is from within, places and things in our past, and in our immediate environment.

THE SIX GHOST FEARS

There are six basic fears, with some combination of which every human suffers at one time or another. Most people are fortunate if they do not suffer from the entire six. Shared here is the Identity in the order of their most common appearance.

The fear of POVERTY

The fear of CRITICISM

The fear of ILL HEALTH

The fear of LOSS OF LOVE OF SOMEONE

The fear of OLD AGE

The fear of DEATH

These fears are at the top of most people's worries.

Analyze yourself

Poverty is not that you are on the street, you can have a desire that you can't meet and you fear not attaining that desire.

Criticism is that, some has criticized you and it has affected your spirit.

Ill health is when the doctor says that you are sick or suffering and you are affected and stuck in it.

Loss of love of someone is merely when you have lost the person that you love and it is or was very hard to make it through the loss.

Old age is when a person fears old age.

Death is when a person fears death.

I felt that this was important to share because after discovering this while reading Napoleon Hill's "Think and Grow Rich and Law of Success," I personally found myself in four of the six fears. If you are not where you desire to be in life you may be experiencing one or more of these fears unconsciously.

Which of the Six Ghost of fears do you struggle with?

_____
_____
_____
_____
_____
_____

Describe situations when you deal with fear

_____
_____
_____
_____
_____
_____
_____
_____
_____
_____
_____
_____
_____

What goals do your fears keep you from achieving?

_____
_____
_____
_____
_____
_____
_____
_____
_____
_____
_____
_____
_____
_____

Don't quit

When things go wrong, as they sometimes will,
When the road you're trudging seems all uphill,
When the funds are low and the debts are high,
And you want to smile, but you have to sigh,
When care is pressing you down a bit
Rest if you must, but don't you quit.

Life is queer with its twists and its turns,
As everyone of us sometimes learns,
And many a failure turns about
When they might have won, had they stuck it out.
Don't give up though the pace seems slow,
You may succeed with another blow.

Often the goal is nearer than,
It seems to a faint and faltering man,
Often the struggler has given up
When he might have captured the victor's cup;
And he learned too late when the night came down,
How close he was to the golden crown.

Success is failure turned inside out
The silver tint of the clouds of doubt
And you never can tell how close you are,
It may be near when it seems so far;
So stick to the fight when you're hardest hit,
It's when things seem worst that you must not quit!

Write down five reasons not to quit:

_____
_____
_____
_____
_____

Chapter 2:

They called it SLRD

> We also rejoice in our sufferings, because we know that suffering produces perseverance.
> Romans 5:3

In elementary school there were only three females among a bunch of males in all of my main classes. Year after year, the teachers and school officials would say this is SLRD group. This was the group they labeled as Slow Leaning and Reading Disability which is considered to be a form of mental health. As a young child, in the second and third grade, I did not understand what that meant. Then, I finally understood that the system thought I was different. It meant the other students and I had difficulty learning, that we were slow, and that hurt. I felt less than everyone and I felt like people were talking about me and laughing at me. The hurt was deeper than anything I had ever experienced before.

The lack of understanding and the emotional effects of this label have had an effect upon my entire life in ways that I am just beginning to understand and overcome as an adult. I want you to know that when there is a lack of proper communication or a lack of understanding in proper communication, it effects the decisions we make and chances that we take in life. During my early years dancing became my escape from the pain and misunderstanding of SLRD. Dancing was my way of communicating all of the feelings in me, the joy, the pain, and the lack of understanding I felt. The good that came from this is that I discovered my ability to find a comforting peace while dancing, that same peace has kept me through difficult and ungratifying experiences.

"Insecurities, low self-esteem, deception, and getting lost in the crowd – that moment, is when one realizes that your family and friends don't know you."

For me, insecurity and low self-esteem were the results of SLRD. Despite my low-esteem and insecurities, I had to learn how to turn positive and negative situations into something of value or something for good.

In life our goal is to find our truth and to seek our purpose in life despite the good and bad, we must do more than wake up and exist. We have to learn to define our purpose, not by what anyone else wants us to be. After we put in the effort to reach success and obtain the desires of our heart we eventually reach that highpoint in life. This does not come without constant constructive and destructive criticism, judgement and labeling. Labels are common in society so we will always be subjected to them throughout life. Some examples of how we are labeled is when we are told that we are too old or too young or we are too aggressive or we are weak or too meek. Basically, we hear that we are too much or not enough of something at some point in our lives. Understand, the labeler has their own pains and is not aware of the damage being done. Individuals who have seen pain and have suffered from it can cause others pain unknowingly. Analyze and recognize the source. Remember, your life will take various and sudden turns but only to help you with the task of becoming who you are, who you are supposed to be and who you always wanted to be. Your experiences may help another person find their path. In life, you will encounter many situations, people and circumstances that may slow or impede your progress but you should expect and welcome such challenges because this is how we grow and learn from each experience.

More often than not, you do not learn everything in life easily and there will be some painful experiences on the journey, these are called life lessons.

Those of us who has experienced life lesson tend to know what it is like to be hurt. Those are the ones who are there to help others through their pain. Those who have learned to discover self and know that we are all humans with limitations, their life is sometimes more practical, those people are usually very passionate about life. We prefer not to suffer through any situation but it is a reality that the suffering does do us many favors. It gives us the important life lessons that shape us and makes us stronger. Those people have a heart that understands the pain of other people. The pain allows us to see the world as it is at times. Once we empty our head and heart from all the negative things, we can fill ourselves with the things that we will cherish like sweet memories, love, compassion, and nature. All of our troubles can turn in our favor if we take time to examine the issue, see the good and love ourselves through the process.

"Loving oneself isn't hard when 'yourself I' is. It has nothing to do with the shape of your face, the size of your eyes, the length of your hair or the quality of your clothes. It's so beyond all of those things and it's what gives life to everything about you. Your own self is such a treasure."
– Phylicia Rashad.

Every day of your journey is an opportunity to make progress in the direction of your dreams and your destination which is the objective of your life. Many people will assist you along this path by helping you realize how to open up to yourself and how to discover yourself but it is you who has to walk the path of your destiny. You have to know that you are a human and you have to face your limitations every single day and confront your fears on a regular basis, this is something that has to be done in order to learn from the experiences of life. Every single day of your life is a platform for you to make some progress in the right direction towards your destiny, your purpose and it will get a little closer and clearer to you than yesterday.

Chapter 3:

Moving Into Life:

Follow Your Passion

> Where your talents and the needs of the world cross, there lies your purpose.
> -Aristotle

In 1986 I started college at West Virginia State University where I studied business management. I felt good about the accomplishment of being accepted into an institution of higher learning. This was my first time away from home and I was excited about the possibilities. This was an opportunity for a new beginning. I met a lot of new people, made new friends and had many great experiences. My first year taking 15 credit hours was a major adjustment. The class work was easy at first. Then, the work became more difficult, once again causing me to question my abilities to succeed and brought back memories of being labelled SLRD. Not only was school becoming more challenging, I received news that my family dynamic was changing dramatically. My parents had decided to separate, and that traumatized me. I lost what was left of my focus and the little interest that I had for the study of business management died. It was during this time that I fell back to the trade I became familiar with while being with my babysitter while she styled hair at Davis Barber and Beauty Salon on Southern Ave in Southeast DC. My dorm was my salon I would have clients 3 to 4 times a week. I became known as the best kitchen beautician on and off campus.

Campus Sweetheart

Although my life seemed to be presenting major problems, I still had some good times. A few of my friends and I decided to become Kappa Sweethearts, an organization associated with the brothers of Kappa Alpha Psi fraternity. For four and a half weeks we showed our loyalty to the Kappa's. This was a great bonding opportunity and a time of growth, it also helped me to forget some of my troubles. At this time I had something to look forward and be a part of in the Kappa Sweethearts. One positive life treasure I carry with me today is:

"Excuses are tools of the weak and incompetent. They were built on monuments of nothingness. Those who excel in it seldom excel in anything else but excuses." -Unknown

I stayed in school for two and a half years and realized that college was not working for me. I was not focused and being a part of the party was more appealing than my studies. During that time I had many experiences that were not allowed in my home. Drinking and smoking were rites of passage, staying up all night seemed standard. College was not working for me. The agreement with my mother was to stay in school at least 2 years. I had done that and I decided it was time to leave the university. I went back to live with my mother. Not as the child that had left her almost 3 years earlier. I returned home as an experienced young woman who had learned to stand on her own and learned, what I thought were my own lessons in life.

One thing that I found at West Virginia University was my passion for cosmetology. To follow my passion I enrolled in Scanners Beauty School in Washington, DC. Elizabeth Nolan was the owner and became a beauty industry mentor. I completed the programs in 9 months and started working at David's Barber Shop on the corner of Southern Avenue and South Capitol Street, the very place I frequented with my babysitter as a child. I was home. My business was growing strong. My clients shared my information with their friends and family. I could see the future in the beauty industry. One of the beauty supply salesman Mr. Al Dudley, Jr. came to the salon. He talked with us all about the hair university and invited me to meet with other stylist for more information about this opportunity. Going back to school was not on my radar, but I attended. There I met Alfred "DeGreat" Dudley, Sr. He was the director of Dudley Beauty College-Washington, a Dudley Sales Manager and the brother of the Dudley brand founder. Mr. Dudley helped to open our eyes to the possibilities in the industry. They discussed being a celebrity stylist, being a salon owner, being a beauty expert. This was excited me and unleashed passion in me. The program to attend Dudley Cosmetology University in Kernersville, NC was introduced. The cost was $1295.00 for 5 days. I was ready to walk out the door at that moment. Mr. Dudley said "wait, I know that the price may scare some people, but I'm going to work with you so that not one dime will come out of your pocket." That is exactly what he did. He setup a program where I retailed products to my clients. All of the profit from the sell of the product went to my education, like an education savings account. In less than 2 months I was North Carolina bound.

How do you develop the power to believe in yourself, to think success, to stop thinking failure, when failure is everywhere that you are – in your home, your car, at work?

I have learned that when difficult situations present themselves, I have to recondition my mind and say that I can overcome this, I can win. Not only to myself but especially to the others who interject their ideas, their opinions and their visions in my life. Those people are unconsciously taking me off the path that God is guiding me on. I have to replace the possibility of losing with the promise of success. I am always reminding myself that I am equal. I have to dispel feelings of being out classed or less. And so do you.

It was at Dudley Cosmetology University, better known as DCU, I was introduced to this way of thinking. I met Dr. Joe L. Dudley, Sr. one of the founders of the Dudley Brand and he changed my life. Dr. Dudley became one of my mentors and he encouraged me to tell myself "I AM, I CAN and I WILL!" Reciting these words to myself, has played and continues to play a very vital role in helping me to believe that success is a very real possibility for my life in whatever I endeavor. I WILL SUCCEED now this dominates my thought process.

Every one of us is a human and we know how that our life is important. The idea and the realization that none of us is perfect is what make us human. The deeper we go into the spiritual world of life; we realize that we know very little about life all this time. It is like when one thinks that you have reached to the top of one mountain you realize that this is just the bottom of the next one. And while we climb our way up through our life we find out what was really important and how all the occasional pain and suffering helped us to be strong enough to make this climb. We can make progress toward power, peace, purpose and prosperity as we free ourselves from the prisons in our mind. We can all progress faster if we remove the obstacles, by becoming mentally free.

In order to feel mentally free I will:

_____
_____
_____
_____

We have all tried to live our life from the outside. What society says or our family says. While all we need to do is to live from the inside. Before we achieve success, we first go through some very hard times and life takes its toll on all of us. At times you can't seem to find the end to all your troubles, but as it is said, we learn the biggest truths from the greatest challenges.

Every challenge, every struggle, every pain that you experience will give you the ability to be stronger than you were before. Life's greatest moments are when you obtain the personal growth that you need for the highest success and it transforms you in a very positive way.

By going through the challenges, victories and hardships you finally reclaim the potential that you once held, you get back to your true power, your peace and true strength. Therefore, instead of running from the pain and suffering embrace it, as these are the moments you learn from. Make no mistake about it; the lows of your life are the stepping-stones towards your purpose and your destiny.

Glass house

A glass house is what I see
Beauty is what I look for within everyone I see
A Glass house can help us to see reflection to view ourselves differently as if it was a mirror
We need to be able to look a little closer in our own lives.
We need to see our negative things as a learning experience and the need to change to positive.
But to see is to understand and to understand is to go back to the values that we were taught from our parents when we were kids.
So if we sweep around your own front door before you sweep around others,
We'll be able to focus on our own. Take 6 months to focus on your own and six months to leave others alone.
My vision is what I see, it will allow me to be me to be the best that I can be
I want to change my life
I want to share my life
I want to build me life
I want my vision to be seen to help those in need.

-Felicia L. Pollard

> My Rock
> You placed a foundation of God in me
> that I will always follow. The
> appreciation and love I have for you will
> forever be.

My Strength
You taught me how to endure with resilience. Keeping me focused on stability in my life

The shoulders on which I stand

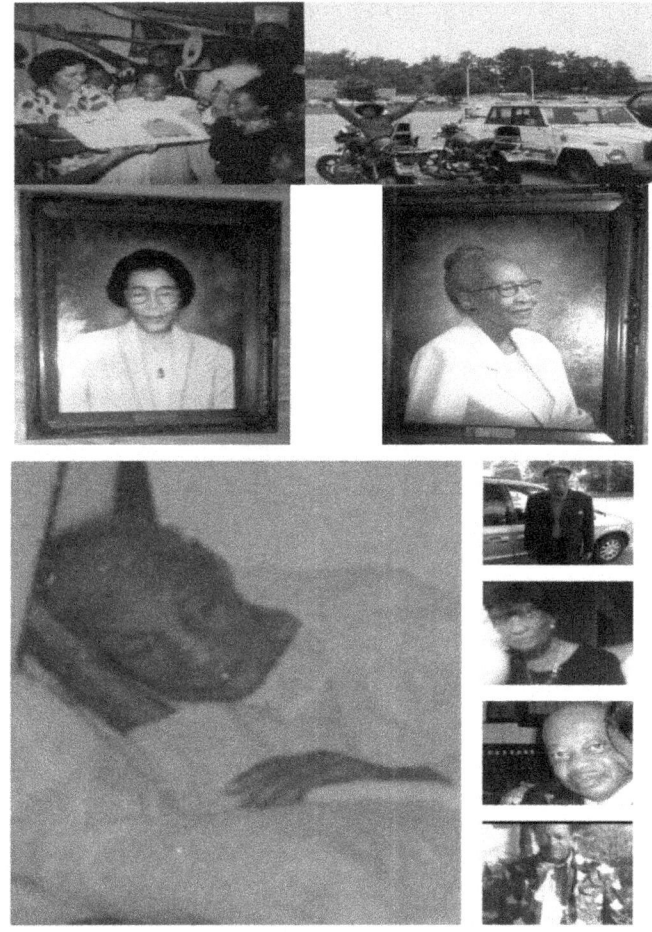

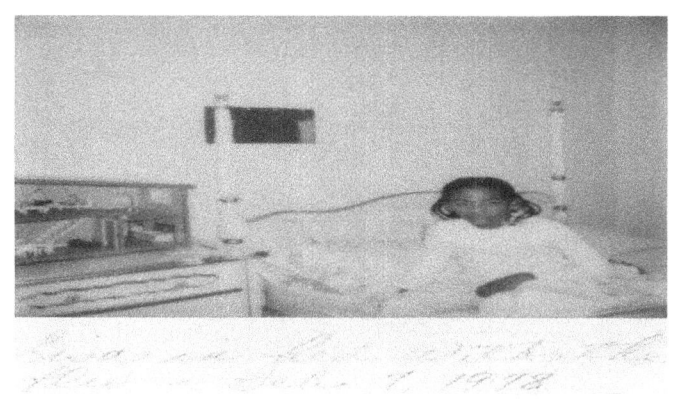

I honor my Husband, my Soulmate

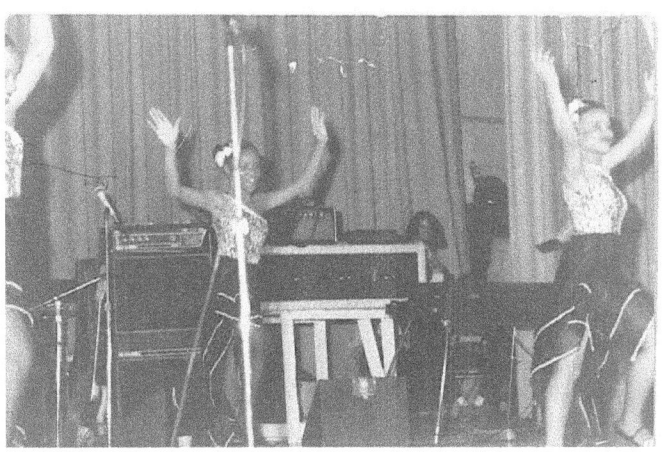

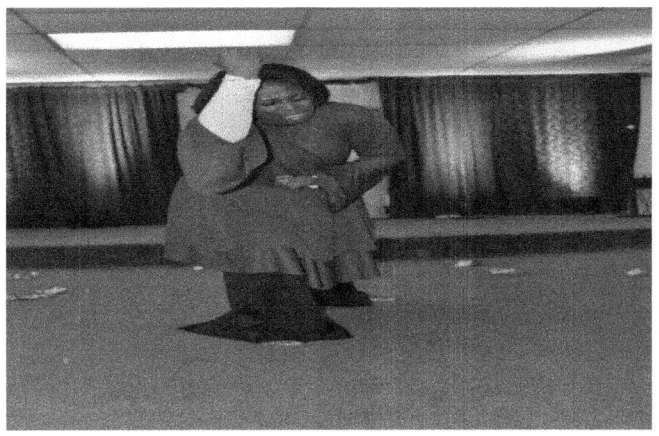

My passions manifest themselves in many ways. Life as a Dudley Educator

Chapter 4:

On the Road to Prison

> As a prisoner for the Lord, then, I urge you to live a life worthy of the calling you have received.
> Ephesians 4:1-6

After dropping out of college, three failed relationships and a lot of disappoint, I reconnected with an old flame. I saw promise in the relationship and then it ended. That occurred along with the separation in my parent's marriage which I admired, desired and aspired to have one day. The series of loss devastated my life and I began to tail spin. I struggled to see my self-worth and life's value. I turned to drugs, actually crack cocaine, as I thought it would ease the pain that I felt. The drug acted like a friend and an escape from my reality. My reality consisted of more than just me, my family was worried about me, because my actions were out of character and against everything that they had instilled in me. I became a disappointment. My family came together and held an intervention. My two great aunts felt a change of environment would put me back on track. It was the late 90's and I was shipped off to a rehabilitation program in Georgia for several weeks. Rehab taught me that I was not alone nor in control. I learned the twelve steps and the serenity prayer.

> "God grant me the serenity to accept the things I cannot change, the courage to change the things I can and the wisdom to know the difference."
> -Karl Paul Reinhold Niebuhr

I was grateful to my family for caring and loving me enough to intervene, I could never repay them for what they spent and did to try to help me. Truthfully, my fears and insecurities had controlled me, people had controlled me and now the drug was controlling me.

Although my family tried it was still something in me that wasn't done with crack. I still remember one of the guys in the crew when I started getting high, he told me that when I get to the point that I am no longer controlling the drug is controlling me and that means, "it got me." Let me explain something. I went to work all day, every day, we all did. At night we came together with our contribution, we bought our product, we would smoke and talked about life. We weren't in the streets, we weren't robbing our parents to pay for our addiction. We were functioning addicts.

My family set me up in an apartment when I graduated from rehab. For the first time I truly had adult responsibilities. The normal adult bills; rent, utilities, and food. I found work in a salon but it takes time to build clientele, not to mention, a business in a new city. Funds were short. I had a life style that I had become accustomed to and the expenses continued, as they do and I had to pay them. I wanted my family to be proud of me. After all they had spent so much time and money trying to help me. I didn't have any money to pay my way so when some friends told me about a shoplifting scheme, I took the bait. That was the shift in my life.

It was a hot Georgia day when I walked into the clothing store thinking that all eyes were on me. I started to leave, I was terrified but I needed the cash and thought I could pull it off. I had gotten away with it. My first lift was a shirt and pants. I returned it to the store, INSTANT CASH. The rush was real. The scheme went on for a few weeks before I was introduced to the forgery game by another group of people. This was my upgrade, there was less risk or so I thought.

My new associates were in the forgery game. I shopped everyday with stolen checks. This was much easier. It kept me off the streets and fuelled my drug habit. For an entire year I thought this was good, life was good. I considered this my job. My family did not have a clue what I was doing to make money. They thought I was in the streets doing drugs, but never anything like this, never stealing. I knew forgery could cause me jail time and eventually did but like we've always heard desperate times call for desperate measures. The other side to that is do not do the crime, if you can't do the time. I would eventually have to pay up. For now, forgery was the hustle. Party at night, get me a piece and go get a room. That was my daily grind. My grind came to a screeching halt.

One day I was in a hotel and the police was there looking for someone else. They burst in and searched the room and found the stolen checks. They hauled me off to jail. I called my mother and she told me she had been praying and God told her to leave me there because she was interfering with what He was trying do in my life. She was my mother she did not want to see her baby in such a state so any time before now she rescued me but this time was different she had instruction from the very One she prayed to. She had to leave me and pray me out of my situation. I had to trust God. It was over a year for my court date. While I waited for sentencing I resided at Fulton County Jail in Georgia. It was there I found that I was in the wilderness. The living conditions were not anything like the life I lived. In this miniature cell was a set of bunk beds, a toilet and a sink all behind bars. I remember one day it was very rainy and the rain dripped in the cell where I sat. This wilderness was just beginning and I fell into a depression. I cried for three weeks in bed. I was so disappointed in myself. The medical staff wanted to give me anti-depressants. It was time to call home. I told my great aunt what the medical plan was for me and she told me not to take the medication but to pray. So I did. My prayers and peace came in the form of writing and dancing. Fulton County Jail is where I found out I needed to dance spiritually. Dance was my first love and I hadn't danced since the Tiny Bubbles. After sitting at Fulton County and all my past had caught up with me I was sentenced to 5 years for all my convictions that ran concurrently from every county that I had been.

In the middle of the night my name was called and I was transported to the transitional center specifically for moving from the jail population to the prison population. It was like a processing center and boot camp training all in one. We had to run, exercise; we were tested medically and became just a number. After three to four weeks we were transported to various prisons. I went to Pulaski State Prison in Hawkinsville, Georgia a medium security institution. That is where I continued my five year sentence.

In Prison one of the first people I met was Amanda. She was an older lady in her fifties who has since passed on. She was one of my lifesavers, she had a good heart. She helped me to learn the inner workings of the prison and how to survive. She taught me that "an even swoop is not a swindle and fair exchange is not a robbery." That means, if you do something for me and I do something for you then the debt is paid. I thought that was profound. I followed her and asked her to repeat that statement day in and day out. I still live by that phrase. I joined the choir and attended church to keep myself occupied. I was seeking God and it was there that I saw lives change and realized that I had a gift. Prison was my rehab. When the warden found out I was a licensed hairstylist she gave me a job in the prison salon after working in the fashion and apparel department where I sowed the prison uniforms. This helped me to sharpen my skills as a stylist. I had the ability to change the way these ladies saw themselves. It was and still is very important to me that women feel their best. I was becoming my true self and saw reward in that. As a result of my constant progress, I was moved to the honor's dorm. This was perfect for me because I am majority introvert. There I had more privacy and privilege. Being there allowed me to focus on where I was going when I left there. I started to plan my life. I developed businesses that have grown into reality. I finally did not have any distractions and I focused on GOD.

It was in prison that I rested. I slept more than I ever had and found peace through my situation which has sustained me since. I did not have moments that I feared for my life.

I did not have to fight or spend time with the stereotypical prison population. The worst part of prison was disappointing my parents and the rest of my family. My mother worried about me every day and actually blamed herself for a while. I knew that I would never knowingly do anything that would cause her pain again. Drugs will make you so selfish, self-centred, and self-seeking so much so that nothing and no one matters. Weather it is crack, marijuana, medication, alcohol, food, shopping, self, material things or status they all can control our lives.

I have learned that we can make our lives worth living and filled with meaningful things that we want to cherish. Man can lock us away, but he cannot lock our minds. We have the power to control our mind when we are mentally well. Therefore, we have to know that we are not victims of life as we create all the moments ourselves by the choices that we make.

Instead of worrying about what life is going to throw at you spend your energy growing from your experiences. Celebrate the challenges while knowing that you have the authority to make your life as beautiful as you want even when imprisoned. The pathway of destiny requires that you go through the process of self-awakening and realize your ultimate truth.

At the end of this chapter:

We have shared facts on mental health, which may help you recognize behaviors and characteristics of yourself and love ones. Don't forget to journal.

I find peace within when I:-
_____
_____
_____

I love myself because:
_____
_____
_____

What Is Mental Health?

Mental health includes our emotional, psychological, and social well-being. It affects how we think, feel, and act. It also helps determine how we handle stress, relate to others, and make choices. Mental health is important at every stage of life, from childhood and adolescence through adulthood.

Over the course of your life, if you experience mental health problems your thinking, your mood, and your behavior could be affected. Many factors contribute to mental health problems, including:

- Biological factors, such as genes or brain chemistry

- Life experiences, such as trauma or abuse

- Family history of mental health problems

Mental health problems are common and people with mental health problems can get better.

Early Warning Signs

Are you not sure if you or someone you know is living with mental health problems? Experiencing one or more of the following feelings or behaviors can be an early warning sign of a problem:

- Eating or sleeping too much or too little

- Pulling away from people and usual activities

- Having low or no energy
- Feeling numb or like nothing matters
- Having unexplained aches and pains
- Feeling helpless or hopeless
- Smoking, drinking, or using drugs more than usual
- Feeling unusually confused, forgetful, on edge, angry, upset, worried, or scared
- Yelling or fighting with family and friends
- Experiencing severe mood swings that cause problems in relationships
- Having persistent thoughts and memories you can't get out of your head
- Hearing voices or believing things that are not true
- Thinking of harming yourself or others
- Inability to perform daily tasks like taking care of your kids or getting to work or school

Mental Health and Wellness

Positive mental health allows people to:

- Realize their full potential
- Cope with the stresses of life

- Work productively
- Make meaningful contributions to their communities

Ways to maintain positive mental health include:

- Getting professional help if you need it
- Connecting with others
- Staying positive
- Getting physically active
- Helping others
- Getting enough sleep
- Developing coping skills

Chapter 5:

Go Walk in Your Purpose: There is Power in Belief

> And we know that all things work together for good to them that love God, to them who are the called according to his purpose.
> Romans: 8:28

I remember thinking and asking God why do I have to go through this? Why do I have to go through so many struggles? It's very interesting one day I asked my brother-in-law the same question. Why me? He said why not you? You're a vessel being used for God. A ball of clay being sculpted in to something beautiful, you will be pulled, pressed and even put into the fire, but when you come out on the other side you are a beautiful purposeful being. I have held on to his words in order to guide and to lead me continuously. I thank God every day for the strength to tackle any obstacles, for the love, and to humbly share and teach others. I am thankful for the faithfulness to stay focused toward my purpose which allows me to follow God each day in honesty. I thank God for the moments of desperation, the inspiration in His word, for the peace and the power that He gave me. God allows me to know that I can be used wherever I am in life. You can be used wherever you are today.

A spiritual journey: Life will happen to you unless you pay attention to life and manage your choices accordingly. -Unknown

Mr. Dudley has told me for years that I had to tell my story. He believes the best way to help yourself is by giving your knowledge to others and helping someone else understand what it is that they should know. Prayerfully my experiences will help you find and understand the deeper wisdom that lies within you.

I believe you should engage in conversation with the people that you love about this and explain the lessons of life that you are experiencing. Share what you are thinking and how it is helping you, let others know of the inside changes that you are going through on a spiritual level. Sharing the thoughts with the people around you will give you the knowledge to a deeper understanding.

Ultimately you will realize your power and purpose.

Normally, when we are facing bad times our thinking reflects the bad time. We repeat the negative situation over and over again. This is similar to uploading negativity to our brain. When it is time to hit play only the negative is present, therefore our action, words and sometimes deeds are negative. Upload good thought to your mind. Catherine Ponder says "Give thanks that the universal spirit of prosperity is providing richly for me now." Say to yourself that "I AM, I CAN, and I WILL."

Sometimes it is your way of looking at things that makes you even sadder or more depressed. The world works something like a mirror to us, if we look at it with sadness it reflects sadness as well. There is beauty in every situation, it's up to you to seek and find the things in this world that bring you peace. I also believe that the times are forever changing and the hard times will not remain with you forever. Every night has its dawn and to see the dawn you should take you burdens to God as He wouldn't put more on you than you can bear.

Most of us are scared of leaving our comfort zone to achieve something greater. We sometimes avoid visiting places we have never been but life takes us to that situation anyway. All of this is fear that we face and we sometimes expect the bad things to happen. Instead we should embrace these situations as a challenge to us and realize that this is the way we are going to fulfill our purpose that holds our future.

You will learn with life's experiences that the world is not a place to be afraid of instead it's the most helpful place for all of your actions, desires, and growth.

It's true a car that never goes on the road and stays in the garage is not going to get damaged. We all know that this is not going to help the car fulfill its purpose either. There was a reason for which the car was built and being set aside, discarded or admired will not bring the car to its purpose.

The same thing can be said for us, we also need to do what we are designed to do. We are made to grow on a personal level with the experiences that we get from the world by meeting new people or by going to new places. A person who does not have a social life and does not talk to anyone cannot get hurt but at the same time we cannot think of that as a way of living a happy and fulfilling life. Our consciousness sees through the pain and troubles that come to us. Our consciousness gives us answers to what we want to know. All the challenges give depth to our thoughts and allow us to open up for what the future has in store for us.

"No structure is complete or secure without the stabilizing power of God – Make Him your Foundation."-Unknown

=The Greatest Power Is In Your Mind

by John Raye

"As long as we allow someone else to control our thoughts, we are in trouble." ---Johnny Robinson, Dudley Products, Fayetteville, NC.

The moment Felicia walked into my 5:00am personal development class dealing with success and personal prosperity; I knew she was, in some strange way, different, perhaps unique in a way that even she didn't quite understand.

In the early 90's I spent four years touring the country with BLACK EXPO USA, a traveling trade show that generated exposure for small Black-owned businesses. It was the place to see and be seen. I was part of a team that conducted business seminars and workshops. In my seminar, I recruited potential participants by promoting a seminar that started at 5:00am and cost $95 to attend.

After explaining what participants would learn during the 2-3 hour session, my rationale went something like this: "If you can't wake up and get up at 5:00 am, then you can't come to my seminar. However, if you wake up but can't come up with $95, you still can't come to my seminar."

During my four year run with Black Expo USA, I never spoke to an empty room. Holding an early morning class at 5am was intriguing, a sure-fire attention getter that drew curious and highly motivated individuals.

I don't know if she paid the $95 or not but this is how and where I first met Felicia. I think I was on staff at Dudley Products where I continued to host the early morning personal development sessions (these sessions were complimentary because I was on staff with the Dudley Products company at the time).

Still, this is where and how I met her and later became her life-long coach and mentor. I taught her what I had been taught, largely about mind control and the critical importance of controlling one's thoughts, words and deeds.

Right away, I noticed she was focused, a good listener with a well-adjusted attitude that matched her spirit. She had an open mind, was thirsty for knowledge and information. Most of all, she had that rare quality--- a teachable attitude.

I taught, most often, from personal experience. Napoleon Hill's "Think and Grow Rich" and the "Law of Attraction" were just two of the many books and reference materials used in my early morning sessions.

In other words, I was doing what such books were instructing us to do, long before I knew what I was doing. Experience, therefore, is the best teacher because you learn twice when you teach yourself.

But like many people, I hardly ever paid any attention to the thoughts that floated in and out of my mind. In my small town, we were taught, largely to: go to church, go to school and go look for a good job.

We knew next to nothing about the development of critical thinking skills or the development of a positive mental attitude. Such attributes as self-love, self-knowledge, self-respect and self-help were rarely discussed in our community. The primary focus was on finding and keeping a good job.

Consequently, I knew more about other people and their problems, than I knew about myself and my problems. I didn't know, for example, that man's greatest power, is his potential to monitor and *control his thoughts* or that every man is little more than the sum total of his thoughts.

I remember how people poked fun and laughed when Muhammad Ali declared himself, "the greatest of all time." Many people, myself included, thought he was just crazy. We'd never heard a Black man call himself, "great," or talk like that before. But he spoke truth to a certain power and lived up to that truth, no matter the outcry and pushback from critics who would later have to eat crow. Ali proved that thoughts and words have *consequences*, and that power is the physical manifestation of all *persistent* thoughts.

It was difficult to ignore him. At one time, his face was, arguably, the most famous face in the world. Though in fading health and out of the public eye for decades, he remains a celebrated icon whose public personae is unlikely ever to be forgotten.

We now know that our words, good or bad, positive or negative, are an outgrowth of our innermost thoughts. And the most *frequent thoughts* we allow to occupy our minds, eventually determines *our destiny*. There is no getting around this universal truth; it is as real as night follows day.

"All that a man becomes or fails to become is directly related to his thoughts… a man can rise no higher than his thoughts, wrote James Allen. I now know, and accept the reality, that I am totally responsible for the thoughts that I allow to occupy my mind.

I have jurisdictional authority over such thoughts. Therefore, I take absolute authority, as well as, *absolute responsibility* for certain thoughts that linger in my mind. I cannot stop them from coming, but I sure can keep from staying or building a bird nest in my mind.

Are you aware of the power embedded in your thoughts? If you don't know, go find someone who does know. Become a student of personal growth and development and learn how to *control* and *manage* yourself.

Thought control is our greatest resource. It is readily available to anyone willing to invest the time, the patience, the energy and *due diligence* required to obtain it. Most people failed to master their thought power simply because of miseducation.

If there's something you don't want in your life, *shut it down!!* Shut it down now! Don's focus, don't think, don't concentrate, don't dwell on what you *don't want!* If you remain steadfast and fixated on the object of your *strongest desire*, you will soon have it!

Come hell or high water, stay the course and keep your eye on the prize. Ignore the naysayers and ankle-biters. Put on your big boy underwear, and *demand* from yourself *exactly* what you want. And that's *exactly* what you will get!

Avoid or ignore people who suggest you, "fake it-until-you-make it." Such advice is given by fools to other soon-to-be-fools. Like Ali, be true to your real self!

So be careful with those thoughts! When you learn to control your thoughts, you really learn how to control your life. And know this much: wherever the mind goes, the feet are sure to follow.

Therefore, I am grateful to be counted among the many foot soldiers that helped to shape, challenge and change the life of this remarkable sister. Her incredible story, why still unfolding, has already yield enough "good fruit" to influence the lives of generations, yet unborn.

May she forever, continue to shine her light, so that others may find their way out of the dark places!

Chapter 6:

Free Yourself from Confinement: Shine Your Light

> 18. Remember ye not the former things, neither consider the things of old. 19. Behold, I will do a new thing...
> Isaiah 43:18-19

All the challenges we go through in our lives make us stronger inwardly. This is the thing that we teach to a young child when he leaves the familiar faces and attends his first day in school with people he is not familiar with. This is scary for the child at first but we all know it is an important step in the series of situations that one has to face in life. The things that you call unknown are also the things that you can think of as new places full of possibilities for you. I have found this to be truth. Not leaving your comfort zone is not good for you, facing the hard times does make your life better. Mr. Dudley always told me that "if you are comfortable then you are not growing. It is in your discomfort that you experience growth."

The challenges also lead you to your path to the greatest goal of your life and only by walking this path will you get to your destiny takes you. Don't fear the unknown; this is the place where you will find the greatest things for your life.

Shine On

Most people spend most of their life within their comfort zone or the place they feel safe, they do not experience life so that they may shine their light and grow into the greatest version of themselves in future.

Some trouble is avoided by doing this but they are also missing out on an opportunity to reach to their full potential and they never really chase their dreams instead they just give up on wishes. I wish I had that promotion. I wish I had a husband or wife. I wish I had this or that, the list is endless.

It is unfortunate a person will quit living for their dreams because they are afraid of getting hurt by failure in the first attempt or because they are too afraid to even begin with the quest for life. They do things as everyone else tells them to and live by the experiences of others. This is not a reason to give up on your life; only death should be the one event that can take the adventures of our lives away.

Start by creating a short list of things that you want to do in your town. Maybe you want to meet the mayor or visit one of those high-end stores. Make a list of five things you want to do and post them on your mirror or put them in your wallet, add them to your notes on your phone or even make it your screen saver. Look at it every day. Say yes to a new life, to a new beginning.

Hanging on to your safety zone in a familiar environment and among familiar faces is exactly like being in a prison of your own fears and worries. The worst part is that most of the time you don't even realize that you are living in a cage built by you, instead you feel like you are free in every manner.

Believe me, I've been on both sides. If you are not stepping out of your comfort zone, meeting new people, living life then you are living in a cage of your own choices with a lie fixed in your head. When you think out of the box and stop following what others say and think for you, you will find everything that you need for your light to shine. Many prisoners don't leave the life because this is what they know and are familiar with, anything new scares them even though they have been to prison and know that it takes their freedom away. They chose to remain a prisoner instead of trying to face the fears and walk an unknown path towards a better life. Free yourself and let your light shine.

Conclusion

I think about the love that I have for my family I am truly grateful for the lessons, the morals and the values they instilled in me. It has been truly amazing. When I look back over the 47 years of my life, I thank God for my family starting with my parents because I wouldn't be here without them. Each one has imparted a different piece to my life and I thank God for allowing them to teach me as best as they knew. Every day the lessons are clearer. I didn't understand back then but now I can appreciate having to go out in the yard and picking a switch off the tree. This was a form of punishment to keep me from the pain that they knew the world had waiting for me. I understand how they were trying to protect me from going in the wrong direction. I understood because:

1. They had been where I was going.
2. They had my best interest at heart.
3. They created a foundation for me to understand God, follow God, depend

on God, trust God and in everything give thanks.

I thank my siblings for all they are in my life. For loving me unconditionally even when they didn't think I understood them. Now I know that they were just trying to teach me to be the best that I could be. I thank God for my older sister and my older brother. I think God for my nieces and nephew(s). I thank God for my godparents for being there with all their love and support, for always being my cheerleaders. They have always given words of wisdom teaching me, showing me and giving me positive examples to follow. I thank God for aligning me with guidance through my life. I understand today that He already knew what my life would be. He knew the direction that my life would take and the mistakes I would make. Although He gave me signs, warnings but I simply ignored them. You can feel when something is not right. Sharpen your instincts. I can see how He placed people in my life as angels some are still in my life today. Some were in my life for just moment and others for a season and some for a lifetime. I'm grateful that God opened my eyes so I could turn the negatives in to positives.

When you find out the path of your destiny or discover the purpose of your life, commit to it so that God can take you on the journey of your life that ends with you being where you always seen yourself.

There are a number of things that you receive during this amazing journey; your heart is filled with love, care, peace, joy and greatness. You may not always be able to see how God is controlling your path, but you can always feel something divine in your path to success.

Everyone who goes through this process of self-awakening will be on their way to their destiny which fulfills the purpose of their life. Go for your dreams. Face your fears and discover your destiny. God is always on your side to show you the directions and to help you.

My desire is that you will learn one thing to your life. That you may continue to gain power, find peace, understand your purpose and achieve prosperity.
May God bless you and make all your days great.

About The Author

Felicia Lewis Pollard is a professional cosmetologist, entrepreneur, beauty advisor, and team leader; make – up artist, non – profit founder and educator. She possesses an extensive background in the beauty industry that spans for more than twenty years. Her goal is to improve the outward appearance of women, while simultaneously enhancing their inner confidence with empowering them through professional cosmetic upkeep.

Pollard started training with Dudley Hair Care Production in 1991, mastered advance training, and platform artistry. She received training at Scanners Beauty Academy in Washington, D.C., The Hair School in Decatur, GA and studied Business Management at West Virginia State. After her extensive training, she served as an educator for Shears of Faith, Bronner Brothers, NuExpressions, Empire Beauty School and Atlanta Technical College. Pollard has also been an instructor teaching: Theory, Chemical Textured Services and phases of hair styling (color, cutting and braiding). In addition, she instructed on skin care, makeup, waxing and aromatherapy. Pollard is a regular hair expert on the syndicated radio show "It's A Matter of Health" hosted by Dr. Veita Bland.

As a leading educator in the cosmetology marketplace, Pollard reigns in her assignment as a change agent for God. Pollard is the founder of B.E.E.F.S. International, a non-profit community organization that produces and promotes hair, fashion, educational, talent empowerment and showcases. The show provides a message of permanent change from a negative mind that produces positive lifestyle. Through all of her experiences, she has stayed humble and true to her passion as a natural hair educator and stylist.

Currently, Pollard is sharing her wealth of experience as a highly successful entrepreneur, stylist and independent contractor for Dudley Products. Pollard is pursuing a bachelor degree and Trichology certification graduating both in 2016.

When we can see beneath the evil all the
golden grains are good
We can love each other better when we are
better understood
                    -Unknown